CHINESE CHARACTERS FOR BEGINNERS

初 學 漢 字

Lo Chiung-yu

PANDA MEDIA CO., LTD.

PANDA MEDIA CO., LTD.

3F, No.153, Ting Chow Rd. Sec.3,
Taipei, Taiwan, R. O. C. 100
Tel: 886-2-2365-3976
Fax: 886-2-2369-1206
E-mail: pandamedia@seed.net.tw

First printing, August 2002
Second printing, December 2002

ISBN 986-80507-0-7

CONTENTS

1	人	rén	19	田	tián	37	看	kàn
2	大	dà	20	力	lì	38	相	xiàng
3	天	tiān	21	男	nán	39	心	xīn
4	日	rì	22	文	wén	40	自	zì
5	月	yuè	23	交	jiāo	41	身	shēn
6	明	míng	24	立	lì	42	口	kǒu
7	女	nǚ	25	夫	fū	43	加	jiā
8	子	zǐ	26	安	ān	44	如	rú
9	好	hǎo	27	字	zì	45	合	hé
10	小	xiǎo	28	家	jiā	46	向	xiàng
11	少	shǎo	29	父	fù	47	門	mén
12	多	duō	30	母	mǔ	48	間	jiān
13	木	mù	31	老	lǎo	49	問	wèn
14	林	lín	32	手	shǒu	50	們	men
15	休	xiū	33	友	yǒu	51	工	gōng
16	本	běn	34	耳	ěr	52	左	zuǒ
17	果	guǒ	35	取	qǔ	53	右	yòu
18	李	lǐ	36	目	mù	54	上	shàng

#	字	拼音	#	字	拼音	#	字	拼音
55	下	xià	71	行	xíng	87	東	dōng
56	火	huǒ	72	回	huí	88	西	xī
57	光	guāng	73	王	wáng	89	南	nán
58	山	shān	74	白	bái	90	北	běi
59	水	shuǐ	75	分	fēn	91	一	yī
60	石	shí	76	衣	yī	92	二	èr
61	土	tǔ	77	角	jiǎo	93	三	sān
62	生	shēng	78	高	gāo	94	四	sì
63	氣	qì	79	美	měi	95	五	wǔ
64	雨	yǔ	80	買	mǎi	96	六	liù
65	電	diàn	81	我	wǒ	97	七	qī
66	魚	yú	82	有	yǒu	98	八	bā
67	馬	mǎ	83	算	suàn	99	九	jiǔ
68	象	xiàng	84	筆	bǐ	100	十	shí
69	出	chū	85	教	jiào			
70	去	qù	86	中	zhōng			

PART3 TEST YOURSELF (MATCHING EXERCISES & PINYIN PRACTICE)

PART4 CD-ROM GUIDELINES

**PART
1**

INTRODUCTION TO CHINESE CHARACTERS

The Evolution of Chinese Characters

Chinese characters evolved over a period of more than five thousand years. In the beginning, the characters were pictographs which originated from pictures of objects in daily life. They gradually evolved as follows:

Pictures

Inscriptions on Oracle Bones

Inscriptions on Bronze Vessels

Small Seal Characters

Standard Style Characters

Inscriptions on Oracle Bones (circa 1765-1122 B.C.)

These are the oldest characters found in China. The people in the Shang Dynasty (1600-1066 B.C.) were superstitious. Fortunetellers would drill small holes in tortoise shells or animal bones, heat them until they cracked, and then transform the cracks into inscriptions by carving on the tortoise shells or animal bones.

Inscriptions on Bronze Vessels (circa 1122-249 B.C.)

These are the second oldest characters. The people in the Zhou Dynasty (1066-256 B.C.) used bronze to make vessels which they used in daily life. They would commemorate great events with inscriptions on the vessels.

Small Seal Characters (circa 221-206 B.C.)

The First Emperor of the Qin Dynasty (255-206 B.C.), Qin Shi Huang unified China during this period. Since the characters at that time varied from region to region, the Prime Minister, Li Si proposed to standardize them. The small seal characters were used as the standard of the written language. In the late Qin Dynasty, the characters were transformed into more straight forms for the sake of convenience. These were called the clerical style characters. The following examples show the differences in styles:

Oracle-Bone	Bronze	**Small Seal**	**Clerical Style**	Standard Style	Cursive Style	Running Style

Standard Style Characters (since the Eastern Han Dynasty)

These are the characters we commonly use today. They were simplified from the clerical style characters during the Eastern Han Dynasty (25-220 A.D.). Besides the standard style characters, the cursive style and running style characters came into being one after the other. Since the standard style characters are easier to write, this style is still the most commonly used today. The following examples show the differences in styles:

Oracle-Bone	Bronze	Small Seal	Clerical Style	**Standard Style**	**Cursive Style**	**Running Style**

The Four Ways of Constructing Chinese Characters

The construction of Chinese characters can be categorized as follows:

> **Pictographs**
>
> **Ideographs**
>
> **Logical Aggregates**
>
> **Determinative Phonetics**

Pictographs

Pictographs were the primitive script that originated from pictures. The following characters show examples of pictographs. As time passed, the ancient Chinese found that pictographs could not convey abstract ideas, and ideographs were invented to fill this need.

Ideographs

Ideographs used symbols like lines or dots to indicate abstract ideas that pictographs could not convey. For instance, "one" is written as 一, "two" as 二, "three" as 三, "up" as 上, "down" as 下 and so on. The invention of ideographs increased the number of Chinese characters.

Logical Agreggates

As rapid civilization took place, pictographs and ideographs were no longer adequate for expressing new abstract ideas. To fill this need, logical aggregates were invented. Logical aggregates combined the meanings of two or more elements to form a new meaning. For instance, the character 日 "sun" and the character 月 "moon" were put together to form the character 明, which means "bright".

Determinative Phonetics

Although the invention of logical aggregates increased the number of Chinese characters, they could not give any hint as to their pronunciation. Determinative phonetics were developed to create new characters by combining a determinative element and a phonetic element. With this innovation, the Chinese writing system became complete. The following example shows how this combination works:

Determinative		Phonetic		Compound
木 wood (mù)	+	每 every (měi)	=	梅 prune; plum (méi)

**PART
2**

LEARNING CHINESE CHARACTERS

人   rén   human being;
              person

ㄖㄣˊ

evolution:

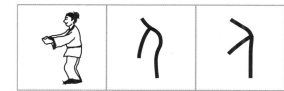

The original form of this character depicted a man standing sidewards with his hands stretching out.

examples:

人口   rénkǒu   population
人類   rénlèi   mankind; humanity
壞人   huàirén   bad person
家人   jiārén   family members
主人   zhǔrén   host; master

stroke order:

2 strokes	人	人	人	人	人	人

1

大　　dà　　big

ㄉ
ㄚ

evolution:

The character shows a man stretching out his arms and legs to the limits, symbolizing "big".

examples:

大家	dàjiā	everyone
大街	dàjiē	main street; avenue
大人	dàrén	adult
大廈	dàshà	big building
大學	dàxué	university

stroke order:

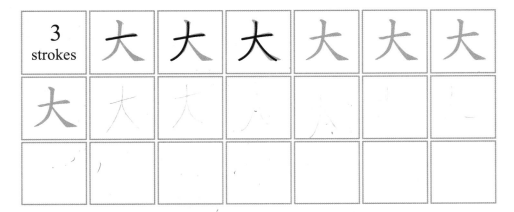

3 strokes

tiān   sky;
               day

ㄊㄧㄢ

evolution:

The top horizontal stroke of the character signifies the sky above a man's head.

examples:

天空	tiānkōng	the sky
天氣	tiānqì	weather
後天	hòutiān	the day after tomorrow
前天	qiántiān	the day before yesterday
昨天	zuótiān	yesterday

stroke order:

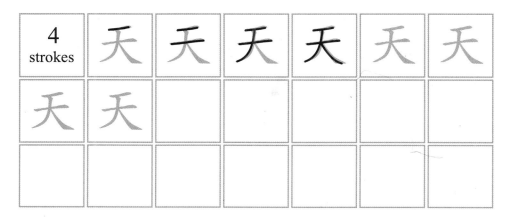

4 strokes

3

日　　rì　　the sun;
　　　　　　day

日ˋ

evolution:

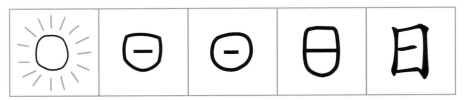

The original form resembled the sun. Since the rising and setting of the sun make a day, this character also means "day".

examples:

日本	Rìběn	Japan
日常	rìcháng	everyday; day-to-day
日記	rìjì	diary
日期	rìqí	date
日夜	rìyè	day and night

stroke order:

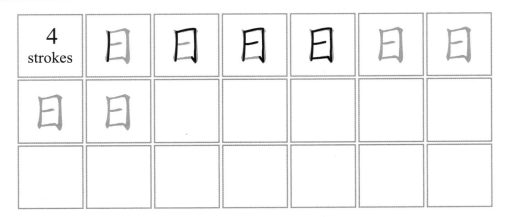

4 strokes

月　　yuè　　the moon; month

ㄩㄝˋ

evolution:

The original form resembled a crescent moon.

examples:

月餅	yuèbǐng	moon cake
月光	yuèguāng	moonlight
月亮	yuèliàng	the moon
月票	yuèpiào	monthly ticket
蜜月	mìyuè	honeymoon

stroke order:

4 strokes	月	月	月	月	月	月
月	月					

míng   bright;
obvious

ㄇㄧㄥˊ

evolution:

The sun and the moon are the brightest objects in the sky. The character 日 "sun" and the character 月 "moon" were put together to form the character 明 "bright".

examples:

明白	míngbái	understand
明亮	míngliàng	bright
明年	míngnián	next year
明天	míngtiān	tomorrow
明顯	míngxiǎn	clear; obvious

stroke order:

8 strokes

nǚ

woman;
female;
girl

ㄋ
ㄩˇ

evolution:

The primitive form depicted a woman kneeling down with her hands resting in front of her chest, a traditional posture in ancient China.

examples:

女ㄋㄩˇ兒ㄦˊ	nǚ'ér	daughter
女ㄋㄩˇ孩ㄏㄞˊ子ㄗ˙	nǚháizi	girl
女ㄋㄩˇ人ㄖㄣˊ	nǚrén	woman
女ㄋㄩˇ生ㄕㄥ	nǚshēng	female student
女ㄋㄩˇ王ㄨㄤˊ	nǚwáng	queen

stroke order:

3 strokes	女	女	女	女	女	女
女						

7

zǐ   son;
       child

ㄗˇ

evolution:

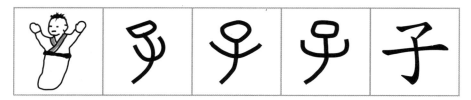

The character resembles an infant waving its arms.

examples:

子ㄗˇ女ㄋㄩˇ	zǐnǚ	sons and daughters (children)
獨ㄉㄨˊ子ㄗˇ	dúzǐ	only son
兒ㄦˊ子ㄗ˙	érzi	son
父ㄈㄨˋ子ㄗˇ	fùzǐ	father and son
孩ㄏㄞˊ子ㄗ˙	háizi	child

stroke order:

3 strokes	子	子	子	子	子	子
子						

好　　　hǎo　　　good

ㄏ
ㄠˇ

evolution:

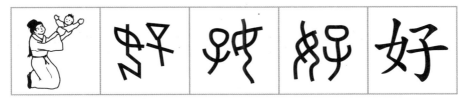

A woman (女) holding a child (子) is a picture of goodness to Chinese.

examples:

好吃	hǎochī	delicious
好處	hǎochù	good point
好看	hǎokàn	pretty; good-looking
好人	hǎorén	good person
好聽	hǎotīng	pleasant to hear

stroke order:

6 strokes	好	好	好	好	好	好
好	好	好	好			

小 xiǎo small

ㄒㄧㄠˇ

evolution:

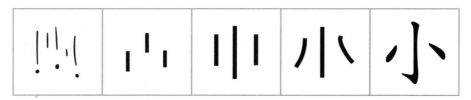

The old form of this character depicted three grains of sand, symbolizing "small".

examples:

小姐	xiǎojiě	Miss; young lady
小時	xiǎoshí	hour
小心	xiǎoxīn	careful; cautious
小學	xiǎoxué	primary school
大小	dàxiǎo	big and small; size

stroke order:

3 strokes	小	小	小	小	小	小
小						

少 shǎo few; little

ㄕ
ㄠˇ

evolution:

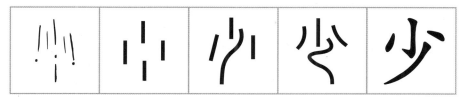

The character 小 "small" combined with the radical ノ, which has the meaning of "to shave off", means to decrease something that is already small.

examples:

少量 shǎoliàng a little; a few
少數 shǎoshù minority
多少 duōshǎo how many; how much
很少 hěnshǎo seldom; very little
減少 jiǎnshǎo decrease; reduce

stroke order:

4 strokes	少	少	少	少	少	少
少	少					

多   duō   many;
           much

evolution:

This character originated from two pieces of meat, and by extension it came to mean "many" or "much". Usually, characters showing two or more objects of the same kind indicate an abundance of that kind of objects, e. g. 林 (forest), 晶 (shining), etc.

examples:

多半	duōbàn	probably; most likely
多虧	duōkuī	thanks to
多數	duōshù	majority
多餘	duōyú	surplus
好多	hǎoduō	many; much

stroke order:

6 strokes	多	多	多	多	多	多
多	多	多	多			

木　mù　　wood;
　　　　　　tree

ㄇㄨˋ

evolution:

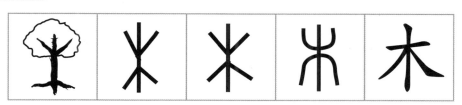

The primitive form resembled a tree with branches and roots. This character originally meant "tree", but its meaning is more often associated with "wood" nowadays.

examples:

木板　　mùbǎn　　board; plank
木材　　mùcái　　timber
木工　　mùgōng　　carpenter; carpentry
木頭　　mùtou　　wood
樹木　　shùmù　　trees

stroke order:

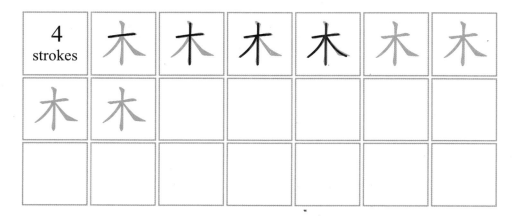

| 4 strokes | 木 | 木 | 木 | 木 | 木 | 木 |

木　木

lín   forest;
grove;
(a surname)

ㄌㄧㄣˊ

evolution:

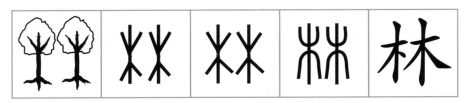

Two trees (木) standing together symbolize a forest.

examples:

林區	línqū	forest area
林業	línyè	forestry
森林	sēnlín	forest
樹林	shùlín	woods; grove
竹林	zhúlín	bamboo grove

stroke order:

8 strokes	林	林	林	林	林	林
林	林	林	林	林	林	

xiū   rest;
           cease

ㄒ
一
ㄡ

evolution:

A person (亻) resting by a tree (木) forms the character 休 "to rest".

examples:

休ㄒ一ㄡ假ㄐ一ㄚ	xiūjià	vacation
休ㄒ一ㄡ息ㄒ一	xiūxí	rest
休ㄒ一ㄡ養一ㄤ	xiūyǎng	recuperate
休ㄒ一ㄡ戰ㄓㄢ	xiūzhàn	cease fire
退ㄊㄨㄟ休ㄒ一ㄡ	tuìxiū	retire

stroke order:

6 strokes	休	休	休	休	休	休
休	休	休	休			

běn   root;
       original;
       book (of blank sheets)

evolution:

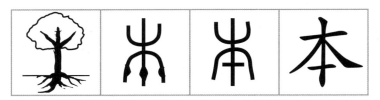

The horizontal short stroke under the character 木 "tree" emphasizes the root from which the tree originates.

examples:

本地	běndì	local; native
本來	běnlái	original; originally
本人	běnrén	oneself; in person
本子	běnzi	notebook
根本	gēnběn	root; basic; fundamental

stroke order:

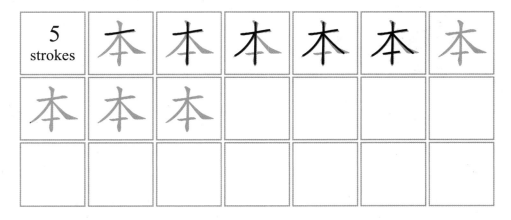

5 strokes

guǒ   fruit;
as expected

evolution:

The old form depicted fruit growing on a tree (木). Avoid confusing the upper part of the character with the character 田 "field" (see p. 19). Its original look is 日, and the long verticle stroke of 木 goes through it. Notice the **stroke order**.

examples:

果醬	guǒjiàng	jam (fruit)
果然	guōrán	as expected
果樹	guǒshù	fruit tree
成果	chéngguǒ	achievement
水果	shuǐguǒ	fruit

stroke order:

8 strokes

 lǐ plum;
(a surname)

力ˇ
一

evolution:

A child (子) under a tree (木) forms the character 李 "plum".

examples:

李樹	lǐshù	plum tree
李子	lǐzi	plum
李先生	Lǐ xiānsheng	Mr. Li
老李	Lǎo Lǐ	Old Li
小李	Xiǎo Lǐ	Little Li

stroke order:

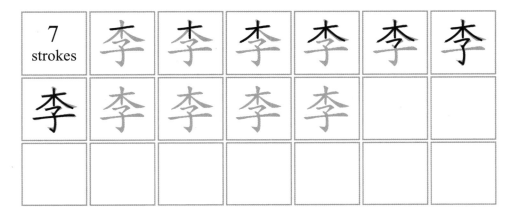

7 strokes

tián   field

ㄊㄧㄢˊ

evolution:

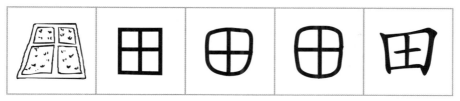

This is a pictograph of a field with furrows.

examples:

田地	tiándì	field
田野	tiányě	open country
田園	tiányuán	countryside; rural area
稻田	dàotián	paddy field
農田	nóngtián	cultivated land

stroke order:

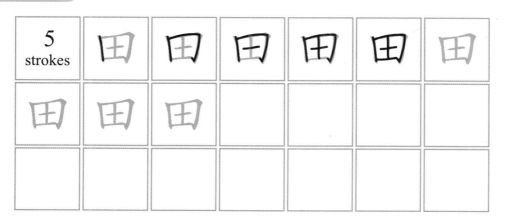

力 lì force; strength

力丶
一

evolution:

The original form of this character depicted an arm, a symbol of physical strength.

examples:

力量	lìliàng	physical strength
力氣	lìqì	effort; strength
吃力	chīlì	difficult; strenuous
努力	nǔlì	make great efforts
人力	rénlì	manpower

stroke order:

2 strokes	力	力	力	力	力	力

男　nán　man;
male;
boy

ㄋ
ㄢˊ

evolution:

In ancient China, it was the duty of men to work in the field. The character 田 "field" and the character 力 "strength" were put together to form the character 男 "man".

examples:

男女	nánnǚ	male and female
男人	nánrén	man
男生	nánshēng	male student
男性	nánxìng	male
男裝	nánzhuāng	men's clothing

stroke order:

7 strokes	男	男	男	男	男	男
男	男	男	男	男		

文　　wén　　script;
　　　　　　　language;
　　　　　　　culture

ㄨㄣˊ

evolution:

The original form depicted a man with tattoos on his chest. This character originally meant "tattoo", but it became a loan character for "script".

examples:

文化　　　wénhuà　　　culture; civilization
文學　　　wénxué　　　literature
文章　　　wénzhāng　　article
文字　　　wénzì　　　　characters; script
日文　　　Rìwén　　　　Japanese language

stroke order:

4 strokes	文	文	文	文	文	文
文	文					

jiāo

cross;
hand over;
associate with

evolution:

The original form of this character resembled a man crossing his legs.

examples:

交叉	jiāochā	crisscross; intersect
交出	jiāochū	hand over
交換	jiāohuàn	exchange
交通	jiāotōng	traffic
交朋友	jiāo péngyǒu	make friends

stroke order:

6 strokes

23

立 lì stand;
establish

ㄌㄧˋ

evolution:

The character depicts a man standing on the ground with his legs apart.

examples:

立場	lìchǎng	standpoint; position
立刻	lìkè	immediately
立體	lìtǐ	three-dimensional
成立	chénglì	establish
起立	qǐlì	stand up

stroke order:

5 strokes	立	立	立	立	立	立
	立	立	立			

夫　fū　husband; man

ㄈㄨ

evolution:

This character depicts a man standing upright with a hairpin in his hair, which was a symbol of adulthood in ancient China.

examples:

夫妻	fūqī	husband and wife
農夫	nóngfū	farmer
懦夫	nuòfū	coward
漁夫	yúfū	fisherman
丈夫	zhàngfū	husband

stroke order:

4 strokes 夫 夫 夫 夫 夫 夫

夫 夫

安　　ān　　peaceful; safe

ㄢ

evolution:

The original form depicted a woman (女) sitting quietly under the roof (宀),
symbolizing "peaceful".

examples:

安ㄢ 靜ㄐㄧㄥ	ānjìng	quiet; peaceful
安ㄢ 排ㄆㄞ	ānpái	arrange
安ㄢ 心ㄒㄧㄣ	ānxīn	at ease
安ㄢ 裝ㄓㄨㄤ	ānzhuāng	install
平ㄆㄧㄥ 安ㄢ	píng'ān	safe and sound

stroke order:

6 strokes	安	安	安	安	安	安
安	安	安	安			

字   zì   character;
                 word

ㄗˋ

evolution:

Children (子) being delivered under the roof (宀) symbolize characters (字) being invented one after the other.

examples:

字ㄗˋ典ㄉㄧㄢˇ	zìdiǎn	dictionary
字ㄗˋ母ㄇㄨˇ	zìmǔ	alphabet
字ㄗˋ幕ㄇㄨˋ	zìmù	subtitle
打ㄉㄚˇ字ㄗˋ	dǎzì	typing
寫ㄒㄧㄝˇ字ㄗˋ	xiězì	writing (words)

stroke order:

6 strokes	字	字	字	字	字	字
字	字	字	字			

家 jiā family; home

ㄐㄧㄚ

evolution:

The radical 宀 "roof" and the old character for "pig" 豕 were put together to form the character 家 "home". In ancient China, every household raised pigs as domestic animals.

examples:

家具 ㄐㄧㄚ ㄐㄩ　　jiājù　　　furniture
家庭 ㄐㄧㄚ ㄊㄧㄥ　jiātíng　　family
家務 ㄐㄧㄚ ㄨ　　jiāwù　　　household duties
家鄉 ㄐㄧㄚ ㄒㄧㄤ　jiāxiāng　　hometown
家長 ㄐㄧㄚ ㄓㄤ　jiāzhǎng　parents

stroke order:

10 strokes	家	家	家	家	家	家
家	家	家	家	家	家	家
家						

父　fù　father

ㄈ
ㄨˋ

evolution:

The original form depicted a hand holding a stone ax, symbolizing "hard working". Usually, the father is the one who works hard to support the family.

examples:

父ㄈㄨˋ母ㄇㄨˇ	fùmǔ	father and mother
父ㄈㄨˋ親ㄑㄧㄣ	fùqīn	father
繼ㄐㄧˋ父ㄈㄨˋ	jìfù	step father
岳ㄩㄝˋ父ㄈㄨˋ	yuèfù	wife's father
祖ㄗㄨˇ父ㄈㄨˋ	zǔfù	paternal grandfather

stroke order:

4 strokes	父	父	父	父	父	父
父	父					

母　　mǔ　　　mother

ㄇㄨˇ

evolution:

The old form of this character depicted a sitting woman with two breasts indicated by two short strokes.

examples:

母ㄇㄨˇ親ㄑㄧㄣ	mǔqīn	mother
母ㄇㄨˇ校ㄒㄧㄠˋ	mǔxiào	alma mater
母ㄇㄨˇ語ㄩˇ	mǔyǔ	mother tongue
伯ㄅㄛˊ母ㄇㄨˇ	bómǔ	aunt
祖ㄗㄨˇ母ㄇㄨˇ	zǔmǔ	paternal grandmother

stroke order:

5 strokes	母	母	母	母	母	母
母	母	母				

lǎo   old

ㄌˇㄠ

evolution:

The original form depicted an old man with a stooped back holding a stick, symbolizing "old".

examples:

老年	lǎonián	old age
老人	lǎorén	the old; the aged
老師	lǎoshī	teacher
老實	lǎoshí	honest
古老	gǔlǎo	old; ancient

stroke order:

6 strokes

老 老 老 老 老 老
老 老 老 老

shǒu　　hand

ㄕㄡˇ

evolution:

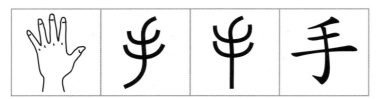

The original form resembled a hand.

examples:

手錶　　shǒubiǎo　　wrist watch
手巾　　shǒujīn　　towel
手術　　shǒushù　　surgical operation
手套　　shǒutào　　gloves
手指　　shǒuzhǐ　　finger

stroke order:

4 strokes

友   yǒu   friend

ㄧㄡˇ

evolution:

This character originated from two right hands close together which symbolized "friendship".

examples:

友好	yǒuhǎo	friendly
友善	yǒushàn	friendly
友誼	yǒuyí	friendship
朋友	péngyǒu	friend
小朋友	xiǎopéngyǒu	little boy or girl

stroke order:

4 strokes	友	友	友	友	友	友
友	友					

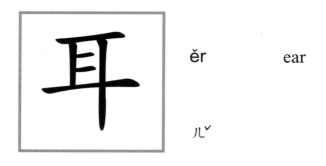

ěr   ear

ㄦˇ

evolution:

The primitive form resembled an ear.

examples:

耳ㄦˇ朵ㄉㄨㄛ	ěrduō	ear
耳ㄦˇ光ㄍㄨㄤ	ěrguāng	a slap on the face
耳ㄦˇ環ㄏㄨㄢˊ	ěrhuán	earrings
耳ㄦˇ機ㄐㄧ	ěrjī	earphones
耳ㄦˇ目ㄇㄨˋ	ěrmù	informer

stroke order:

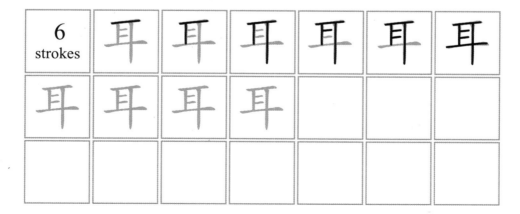

6 strokes

qǔ　　　take;
　　　　　get

くˇ

evolution:

In ancient China, a soldier had to cut off his enemy's ear as proof of his victory. This character shows a right hand (又) taking an ear (耳).

examples:

取代	qǔdài	replace
取得	qǔdé	get; obtain
取消	qǔxiāo	cancel
取笑	qǔxiào	laugh at
争取	zhēngqǔ	strive for

stroke order:

8 strokes	取	取	取	取	取	取
取	取	取	取	取	取	

目　　mù　　　eye

ㄇㄨ

evolution:

The original form resembled an eye. Nowadays, it is more common to use the character 眼 (**yǎn**) to mean "eye" instead of the character 目.

examples:

目標	mùbiāo	target; goal
目的	mùdì	purpose
目光	mùguāng	vision; sight
目錄	mùlù	catalog
目前	mùqián	at present

stroke order:

5 strokes	目	目	目	目	目	目
目	目	目				

kàn   see;
look at

ㄎ
ㄢˋ

evolution:

The original form depicted a man putting his hand (手) above his eyes (目) to see clearly without the sun's rays.

examples:

看病	kànbìng	visit a doctor
看法	kànfǎ	view; opinion
看見	kànjiàn	see
看破	kànpò	see through
看中	kànzhòng	take a fancy to

stroke order:

9
strokes

看 看 看 看 看 看
看 看 看 看 看 看 看

相 xiàng   looks;
            appearance

ㄒ
ㄧ
ㄤ

evolution:

The original form of the character depicted an eye (目) observing a tree (木). This character originally meant "to observe", but it came to mean "looks" or "appearance".

examples:

相本	xiàngběn	photo album
相機	xiàngjī	camera
相貌	xiàngmào	looks; appearance
相片	xiàngpiàn	photograph
照相	zhàoxiàng	take a picture

stroke order:

9 strokes	相	相	相	相	相	相
相	相	相	相	相	相	相

心 xīn heart; mind

ㄒㄧㄣ

evolution:

The original form of this character resembled a heart.

examples:

心情	xīnqíng	state of mind
心臟	xīnzàng	the heart
粗心	cūxīn	careless
點心	diǎnxīn	refreshments; pastry
灰心	huīxīn	disheartened

stroke order:

4 strokes 心 心 心 心 心 心 心 心

自　　zì　　self;
　　　　　　oneself

ㄗˋ

evolution:

This character meant "nose" originally. It came to mean "oneself" since a man usually points to his nose to refer to himself when talking.

examples:

自ㄗˋ動ㄉㄨㄥˋ	zìdòng	automatic
自ㄗˋ己ㄐㄧˇ	zìjǐ	oneself
自ㄗˋ滿ㄇㄢˇ	zìmǎn	self-satisfied
自ㄗˋ私ㄙ	zìsī	selfish
自ㄗˋ由ㄧㄡˊ	zìyóu	freedom; liberty

stroke order:

6 strokes

shēn   body

ㄕㄣ

evolution:

The character originally depicted a pregnant woman standing sidewards, and by extension it came to mean "body".

examples:

身ㄕㄣ 邊ㄅㄧㄢ   shēnbiān   at one's side
身ㄕㄣ 材ㄘㄞ   shēncái   figure; body shape
身ㄕㄣ 高ㄍㄠ   shēngāo   height
身ㄕㄣ 體ㄊㄧˇ   shēntǐ   body
身ㄕㄣ 心ㄒㄧㄣ   shēnxīn   body and mind

stroke order:

7 strokes	身	身	身	身	身	身
身	身	身	身	身		

口　　kǒu　　mouth;
　　　　　　　opening

ㄎ
ㄡˇ

evolution:

This is a pictograph of a mouth.

examples:

口ㄎㄡˇ袋ㄉㄞˋ	kǒudài	pocket
口ㄎㄡˇ紅ㄏㄨㄥˊ	kǒuhóng	lipstick
口ㄎㄡˇ渴ㄎㄜˇ	kǒukě	thristy
口ㄎㄡˇ試ㄕˋ	kǒushì	oral examination
開ㄎㄞ口ㄎㄡˇ	kāikǒu	open one's mouth; talk

stroke order:

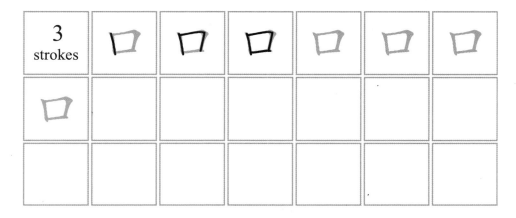

3
strokes

jiā   add;
       increase

ㄐ
ㄧ
ㄚ

evolution:

When strength (力) is added to mouth (口), force is added to words. This character originally meant "to strengthen an argument by adding words", and it finally came to mean "to add".

examples:

加ㄐㄧㄚ班ㄅㄢ   jiābān   work overtime
加ㄐㄧㄚ倍ㄅㄟ   jiābèi   double
加ㄐㄧㄚ法ㄈㄚ   jiāfǎ   addition (mathematics)
加ㄐㄧㄚ強ㄑㄧㄤ   jiāqiáng   strengthen
增ㄗㄥ加ㄐㄧㄚ   zēngjiā   increase

stroke order:

5 strokes	加	加	加	加	加	加
加	加	加				

rú   in compliance with;
                      as if

口
ㄨˊ

evolution:

A master's mouth (口) which gives orders, and a woman (女) who obeys him were combined to form the character 如 "in compliance with".

examples:

如此	rúcǐ	so; in such a way
如果	rúguǒ	if
如同	rútóng	similar to; as if
如下	rúxià	as follows
如意	rúyì	as one wishes

stroke order:

6 strokes	如	如	如	如	如	如
如	如	如	如			

 hé close;
join

evolution:

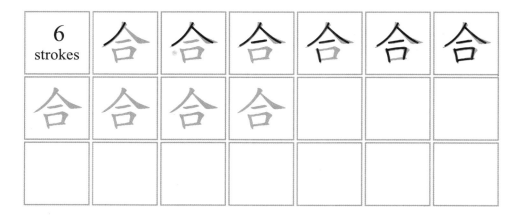

This character resembles a lid and a container joined together, symbolizing "to join".

examples:

合唱	héchàng	chorus
合力	hélì	join forces
合攏	hélǒng	close up
合身	héshēn	fit (clothes)
合作	hézuò	cooperate

stroke order:

6 strokes	合	合	合	合	合	合
合	合	合	合			

向　xiàng　direction;
　　　　　facing;
　　　　　toward

evolution:

A roof (宀) and an opening (口) were combined to form the character 向. This character originally depicted a house facing north, and it finally came to mean "facing" or "direction".

examples:

向 來　　xiànglái　　always
向 前　　xiàngqián　　toward the front
向 上　　xiàngshàng　　face upward
動 向　　dòngxiàng　　direction of movement
方 向　　fāngxiàng　　direction

stroke order:

6 strokes	向	向	向	向	向	向
向	向	向	向			

門
mén   door;
gate

evolution:

This is a pictograph of a traditional Chinese door.

examples:

門口	ménkǒu	doorway
門牌	ménpái	house number
門票	ménpiào	admission ticket
門診	ménzhěn	outpatient service
大門	dàmén	gate

stroke order:

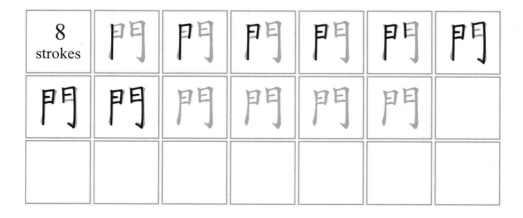

8 strokes						

間

间
jiān

within a definite space or time;
between;
room

ㄐ
一
ㄢ

evolution:

The character 間 was originally written as 閒, which depicted viewing the moon (月)
through a door (門), indicating a definite space and time.

examples:

房ㄈㄤ 間ㄐㄧㄢ	fángjiān	room
空ㄎㄨㄥ 間ㄐㄧㄢ	kōngjiān	space
時ㄕ 間ㄐㄧㄢ	shíjiān	time
中ㄓㄨㄥ 間ㄐㄧㄢ	zhōngjiān	between; in the middle
洗ㄒㄧ 手ㄕㄡ 間ㄐㄧㄢ	xǐshǒujiān	rest room; toilet

stroke order:

12 strokes

48

問
问
wèn   ask;
           inquire
ㄨㄣˋ

evolution:

Since inquiries are usually made at the entrance to a house, the character 門 "door" and the character 口 "mouth" were put together to form the character 問 "to inquire".

examples:

問答	wèndá	questions and answers
問路	wènlù	ask for directions
問題	wèntí	question; problem
訪問	fǎngwèn	visit; interview
學問	xuéwèn	learning; knowledge

stroke order:

11 strokes

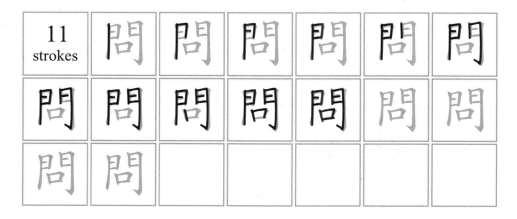

们
men (plural suffix)

evolution:

This character has the radical 亻 "person" as a symbol and the character 門 (men) "door" as a phonetic element.

examples:

你们	nǐmen	you; you (plural number)
人们	rénmen	people
他们	tāmen	they; them
學生們	xuéshēngmen	students
我们	wǒmen	we; us

stroke order:

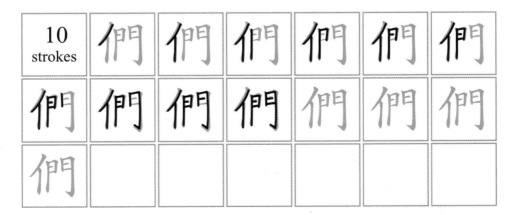

10 strokes

工 gōng work; industry

《ㄨㄥ

evolution:

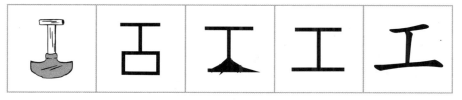

This character is a pictograph of a tool used by ancient workmen. It originally meant "tool", but it came to mean "work".

examples:

工廠 gōngchǎng factory
工具 gōngjù tool
工人 gōngrén worker
工業 gōngyè industry
工作 gōngzuò work; job

stroke order:

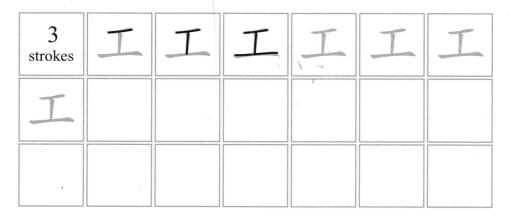

zuǒ   left;
(a surname)

ㄗㄨㄛˇ

evolution:

The character depicts a left hand (ナ) holding a tool (エ), symbolizing "left".

examples:

左邊	zuǒbiān	the left side
左手	zuǒshǒu	the left hand
左翼	zuǒyì	the left wing
左右	zuǒyòu	left and right
向左	xiàngzuǒ	turn left

stroke order:

5 strokes	左	左	左	左	左	左
左	左	左				

yòu   right

ㄧ
ㄡˋ

evolution:

This character depicts a hand (ナ) above a mouth (口), indicating the hand that most people eat with – the right.

examples:

右邊	yòubiān	the right side
右手	yòushǒu	the right hand
右翼	yòuyì	the right wing
向右	xiàngyòu	turn right
左右手	zuǒyòushǒu	right-hand man

stroke order:

5 strokes	右	右	右	右	右	右
右	右	右				

53

shàng   up;
         above

ㄕ
ㄤˋ

evolution:

The original form depicted an object placed on a mat, conveying the abstract idea of "up" or "above".

examples:

上ㄕㄤˋ班ㄅㄢ	shàngbān	go to work
上ㄕㄤˋ課ㄎㄜˋ	shàngkè	attend class
上ㄕㄤˋ來ㄌㄞˊ	shànglái	come up
上ㄕㄤˋ面ㄇㄧㄢˋ	shàngmiàn	above; on top of
上ㄕㄤˋ學ㄒㄩㄝˊ	shàngxué	go to school

stroke order:

3 strokes	上	上	上	上	上	上
上						

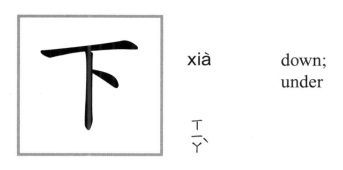

xià   down;
under

ㄒㄧㄚˋ

evolution:

The original form of this character resembled an object placed under a cover, conveying the abstract idea of "down" or "under".

examples:

下班	xiàbān	get off work
下課	xiàkè	finish class
下來	xiàlái	come down
下面	xiàmiàn	bottom; under
下去	xiàqù	go down

stroke order:

3 strokes	下	下	下	下	下	下
下						

火 　huǒ　　fire

ㄏㄨㄛˇ

evolution:

The original form of this character resembled a fire.

examples:

火車	huǒchē	railroad train
火爐	huǒlú	stove (for heating)
火山	huǒshān	volcano
放火	fànghuǒ	set fire
救火	jiùhuǒ	fire fighting

stroke order:

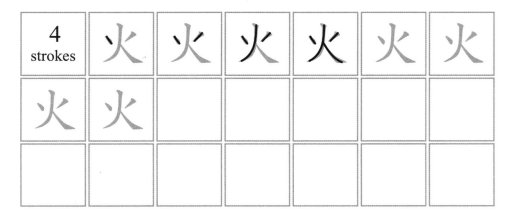

4 strokes

光 guāng light; glory

ㄍㄨㄤ

evolution:

The original form depicted a fire above a kneeling man, symbolizing "light".

examples:

光滑	guānghuá	smooth
光亮	guāngliàng	shiny; bright
光芒	guāngmáng	ray of light; brilliance
光榮	guāngróng	glory; honor
燈光	dēngguāng	lamplight

stroke order:

6 strokes	光	光	光	光	光	光
光	光	光	光			

shān   moutain;
hill

ㄕ
ㄢ

evolution:

This is a pictograph depicting three towering mountain peaks.

examples:

山ㄕㄢ 地ㄉㄧ	shāndì	hilly area
山ㄕㄢ 頂ㄉㄧㄥ	shāndǐng	mountain top
山ㄕㄢ 谷ㄍㄨ	shāngǔ	valley
山ㄕㄢ 坡ㄆㄛ	shānpō	hill slope
山ㄕㄢ 區ㄑㄩ	shānqū	mountainous region

stroke order:

3 strokes	山	山	山	山	山	山
山						

shuǐ   water

evolution:

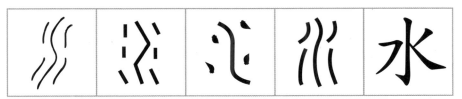

The original form of this character resembled running water.

examples:

水池	shuǐchí	pond; pool
水管	shuǐguǎn	water pipe
風水	fēngshuǐ	geomancy
開水	kāishuǐ	boiled water
汽水	qìshuǐ	soda water; carbonated drink

stroke order:

4 strokes	水	水	水	水	水	水
水	水					

石　shí　stone; rock

ㄕˊ

evolution:

This character depicts a big rock located near a cliff.

examples:

石ㄕˊ頭ㄊㄡ˙　　　shítou　　　stone; rock

石ㄕˊ油ㄧㄡˊ　　　shíyóu　　　petroleum

寶ㄅㄠˇ石ㄕˊ　　　bǎoshí　　　gem

岩ㄧㄢˊ石ㄕˊ　　　yánshí　　　rock

鑽ㄗㄨㄢˋ石ㄕˊ　　　zuànshí　　　diamond

stroke order:

5 strokes	石	石	石	石	石	石
石	石	石				

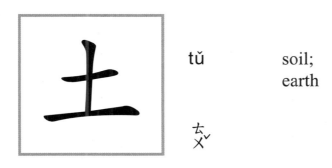

tǔ   soil;
             earth

ㄊㄨˇ

evolution:

The original form of this character depicted a small hill of soil on the ground.

examples:

土產   tǔchǎn   local product
土地   tǔdì   land; soil
土氣   tǔqì   rustic
土人   tǔrén   natives
泥土   nítǔ   soil

stroke order:

3 strokes	土	土	土	土	土	土
土						

shēng   be alive;
give birth to;
produce

ㄕ
ㄥ

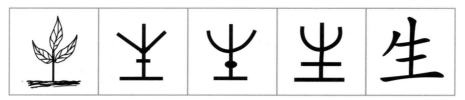

The original form depicted a sprout growing from the earth, a symbol of birth.

examples:

生ㄥ產ㄢ	shēngchǎn	produce; give birth
生ㄥ活ㄜ	shēnghuó	life; livelihood; living
生ㄥ命ㄥ	shēngmìng	life (be alive)
生ㄥ氣ㄧ	shēngqì	get angry
生ㄥ日ㄖ	shēngrì	birthday

stroke order:

5 strokes	生	生	生	生	生	生
生	生	生				

气
qì

く

air;
gas;
make (get) angry

evolution:

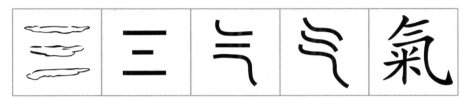

The old form of this character resembled a current of air.

examples:

氣憤   qìfèn   angry; furious

氣候   qìhòu   climate

氣球   qìqiú   balloon

毒氣   dúqì   poisonous gas

空氣   kōngqì   air; atmosphere

stroke order:

10 strokes	氣	氣	氣	氣	氣	氣
氣	氣	氣	氣	氣	氣	氣
氣						

yǔ   rain

ㄩˇ

evolution:

The original form depicted raindrops falling down from the sky.

examples:

雨ㄩˇ傘ㄙㄢˇ	yǔsǎn	umbrella
雨ㄩˇ衣ㄧ	yǔyī	raincoat
雨ㄩˇ鞋ㄒㄧㄝˊ	yǔxié	rain boot
風ㄈㄥ雨ㄩˇ	fēngyǔ	wind and rain
下ㄒㄧㄚˋ雨ㄩˇ	xiàyǔ	raining

stroke order:

8 strokes

電

电
diàn   electricity;
              lightning

ㄅ
ㄧ
ㄢˋ

evolution:

The original form depicted the appearance of lightning in the rain.

examples:

電ㄅㄧㄢ 燈ㄅㄥ   diàndēng   electric lamp

電ㄅㄧㄢ 話ㄏㄨㄚˋ   diànhuà   telephone; telephone call

電ㄅㄧㄢ 器ㄑㄧˋ   diànqì   electric appliance

電ㄅㄧㄢ 視ㄕˋ   diànshì   television

閃ㄕㄢˇ 電ㄅㄧㄢ   shǎndiàn   lightning

stroke order:

13 strokes	電	電	電	電	電	電
電	電	電	電	電	電	電
電	電	電	電			

65

魚
鱼
yú   fish

ㄩˊ

evolution:

The original form resembled a fish.

examples:

魚ㄩˊ竿ㄍㄢ	yúgān	fishing pole
魚ㄩˊ網ㄨㄤˇ	yúwǎng	fishnet
釣ㄉㄧㄠˋ魚ㄩˊ	diàoyú	fishing
金ㄐㄧㄣ魚ㄩˊ	jīnyú	goldfish
鯊ㄕㄚ魚ㄩˊ	shāyú	shark

stroke order:

11 strokes

魚 魚 魚 魚 魚 魚
魚 魚 魚 魚 魚 魚 魚
魚 魚

馬

马
mǎ　　　horse

ㄇㄚˇ

evolution:

The original form of this character resembled a horse.

examples:

馬車	mǎchē	carriage; cart
馬虎	mǎhū	careless; casual
馬路	mǎlù	road; street
馬上	mǎshàng	immediately
騎馬	qímǎ	ride a horse

stroke order:

10 strokes	馬	馬	馬	馬	馬	馬
馬	馬	馬	馬	馬	馬	馬
馬						

象
xiàng

elephant;
appearance

ㄒㄧㄤˋ

evolution:

The original form resembled an elephant.

examples:

象鼻	xiàngbí	elephant's trunk
象棋	xiàngqí	Chinese chess
象牙	xiàngyá	elephant's tusk; ivory
大象	dàxiàng	elephant
現象	xiànxiàng	appearance (of things)

stroke order:

12
strokes

象 象 象 象 象 象
象 象 象 象 象 象
象 象 象

68

chū　　go out;
produce

evolution:

The old form depicted one foot of a primitive man stepping out of his cave, symbolizing "to go out".

examples:

出版	chūbǎn	publish
出產	chūchǎn	produce; manufacture
出口	chūkǒu	exit; export
出門	chūmén	be away from home
出去	chūqù	go out

stroke order:

5 strokes	出	出	出	出	出	出
出	出	出				

去　qù　go; leave

ㄑㄩ

The old form depicted a primitive man leaving his cave, signifying "to go" or "to leave".

examples:

去年	qùnián	last year
去世	qùshì	pass away; die
去向	qùxiàng	trend; whereabouts
進去	jìnqù	go in; enter
上去	shàngqù	go up

stroke order:

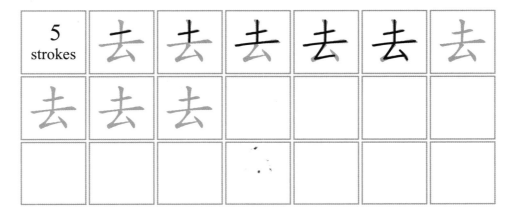

5 strokes

xíng   walk;
         travel

ㄒㄧㄥˊ

evolution:

The original form of this character was a pictograph of a crossroad.

examples:

行李	xínglǐ	baggage
行人	xíngrén	pedestrian
行走	xíngzǒu	walk
流行	liúxíng	be prevalent; be popular
旅行	lǚxíng	travel; take a trip

stroke order:

6 strokes

 huí   return;
              turn around

evolution:

This character resembles water whirling around, symbolizing "to turn around".

examples:

回答	huídá	answer; reply
回國	huíguó	return to one's own country
回家	huíjiā	return home
回來	huílái	return; come back
回去	huíqù	return; go back

stroke order:

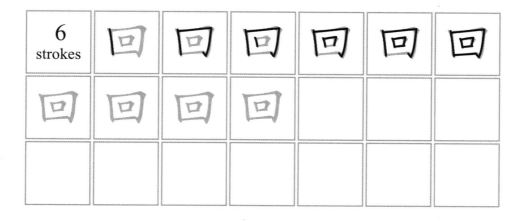

6 strokes

 wáng   king;
                        (a surname)

ㄨ
ㄤˊ

The original form depicted a ruler stretching his arms and legs to the limits between heaven and earth, symbolizing that he ruled everything.

examples:

王ㄨㄤ 宮ㄍㄨㄥ	wánggōng	imperial palace
王ㄨㄤ 國ㄍㄨㄛˊ	wángguó	kingdom
王ㄨㄤ 子ㄗˇ	wángzǐ	prince
大ㄉㄚˋ 王ㄨㄤ	dàwáng	king; magnate
國ㄍㄨㄛˊ 王ㄨㄤ	guówáng	king

stroke order:

4 strokes	王	王	王	王	王	王
王	王					

bái

clear;
white;
(a surname)

evolution:

The character originally depicted the flame of a candle, symbolizing "clear", and by extension it came to mean "white".

examples:

白費	báifèi	in vain; waste
白色	báisè	white
白糖	báitáng	white sugar
白天	báitiān	daytime; day
白雲	báiyún	white cloud

stroke order:

5 strokes

分　fēn　divide; separate

ㄈㄣ

evolution:

Something divided (八) by a knife (刀) forms the character 分 "to divide".

examples:

分別	fēnbié	part; differentiate
分居	fēnjū	live apart
分開	fēnkāi	separate
分類	fēnlèi	classify
分配	fēnpèi	distribute; assign

stroke order:

4 strokes　分　分　分　分　分　分

分　分

yī   clothes

一

evolution:

The original form resembled a garment.

examples:

衣-服	yīfú	clothes
衣-櫃	yīguì	wardrobe
衣-架	yījià	clothes hanger
毛衣	máoyī	sweater
内衣	nèiyī	underwear

stroke order:

6 strokes   衣 衣 衣 衣 衣 衣

衣 衣 衣 衣

jiǎo horn;
corner

ㄐㄧㄠˇ

evolution:

The primitive form resembled an animal's horn.

examples:

角ㄐㄧㄠˇ度ㄉㄨˋ	jiǎodù	angle
角ㄐㄧㄠˇ落ㄌㄨㄛˋ	jiǎoluò	corner
號ㄏㄠˋ角ㄐㄧㄠˇ	hàojiǎo	bugle
牛ㄋㄧㄡˊ角ㄐㄧㄠˇ	niújiǎo	ox horn
牆ㄑㄧㄤˊ角ㄐㄧㄠˇ	qiángjiǎo	wall corner

stroke order:

7 strokes	角	角	角	角	角	角
角	角	角	角	角		

高　　gāo　　high;
　　　　　　　tall

《
幺

evolution:

This character resembles a high tower or pavilion.

examples:

高《大ㄅㄚ	gāodà	tall and big
高《低ㄅㄧ	gāodī	high and low
高《度ㄅㄨ	gāodù	height
高《級ㄐㄧ	gāojí	high class
高《興ㄒㄧㄥ	gāoxìng	happy; delighted

stroke order:

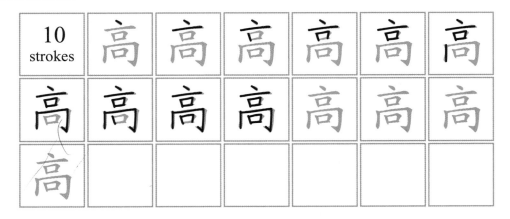

10 strokes

měi   beautiful

evolution:

The old form depicted a man with feathers or animal horns on his head, symbolizing "beautiful".

examples:

美好	měihǎo	good; fine
美麗	měilì	beautiful
美妙	měimiào	splendid; wonderful
美人	měirén	beautiful woman; beauty
美術	měishù	fine arts

stroke order:

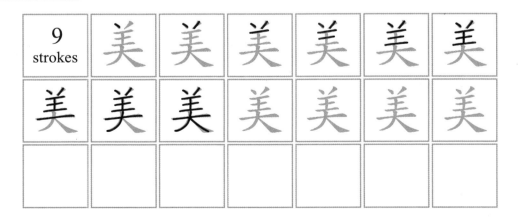

9 strokes

79

买
mǎi   buy

ㄇㄞˇ

evolution:

The character 買 is made up of a net (罒) and a shell (貝). Since shells were once used as business currency in ancient China, to gather shells implied to do business.

examples:

買方	mǎifāng	buyer
買價	mǎijià	buying price
買賣	mǎimài	buying and selling; business
買通	mǎitōng	bribe
購買	gòumǎi	purchase; buy

stroke order:

12 strokes

我   wǒ   I;
me

ㄨㄛˇ

evolution:

This character originally indicated a kind of weapon, but it came to mean "I" or "me".

examples:

我ㄨㄛˇ的ㄉㄜ	wǒ de	my; mine
我ㄨㄛˇ愛ㄞˋ你ㄋㄧˇ	wǒ ài nǐ	I love you
我ㄨㄛˇ們ㄇㄣˊ的ㄉㄜ	wǒmen de	our; ours
忘ㄨㄤˋ我ㄨㄛˇ	wàngwǒ	oblivious of oneself
自ㄗˋ我ㄨㄛˇ	zìwǒ	self

stroke order:

7 strokes	我	我	我	我	我	我
我	我	我	我	我		

有　yǒu　have; possess

ㄧ
ㄡˇ

evolution:

A hand (ナ) holding a piece of meat (月) indicates "to have" or " to possess". The original form of the radical "meat" was 月 , but it was later changed into 月. Be aware of its similarity with the radical 月 "moon".

examples:

有ㄧㄡˇ害ㄏㄞˋ	yǒuhài	harmful
有ㄧㄡˇ名ㄇㄧㄥˊ	yǒumíng	well-known; famous
有ㄧㄡˇ用ㄩㄥˋ	yǒuyòng	useful
沒ㄇㄟˊ有ㄧㄡˇ	méiyǒu	not have; there is not
擁ㄩㄥ有ㄧㄡˇ	yōngyǒu	possess; have

stroke order:

6 strokes	有	有	有	有	有	有
有	有	有	有			

 suàn calculate; count

ㄙㄨㄢˋ

evolution:

The radical 竹 "bamboo" on top indicates what an abacus is made of. The middle part 目 resembles an abacus and the lower part 廾 resembles two hands using it.

examples:

算命 suànmìng fortune telling
算盤 suànpán abacus
算術 suànshù arithmetic
算賬 suànzhàng do accounts; make out bills
計算 jìsuàn calculate

stroke order:

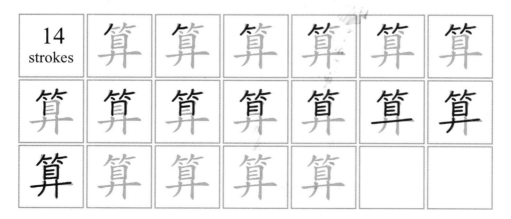

14 strokes

笔
bǐ　　　　pen

ㄅ
ㄧ

evolution:

The character 筆 resembles a hand holding a Chinese brush. The radical ⺮ "bamboo" on top indicates what a Chinese brush is made of.

examples:

筆畫	bǐhuà	stroke of a character
筆記	bǐjì	notes
筆試	bǐshì	written examination
鋼筆	gāngbǐ	fountain pen
鉛筆	qiānbǐ	pencil

stroke order:

12 strokes

jiào   teach;
religion

ㄐㄧㄠˋ

evolution:

The original form depicted a teacher's hand holding a stick, teaching a child.

examples:

教材	jiàocái	teaching material
教導	jiàodǎo	teach; instruct
教師	jiàoshī	teacher
教室	jiàoshì	classroom
教堂	jiàotáng	church (building)

stroke order:

11 strokes

教 教 教 教 教 教
教 教 教 教 教 教 教
教 教

zhōng   middle;
China

ㄓㄨㄥ

evolution:

The original form of this character resembled a flag on a pole standing in the middle of a circle.

examples:

中國	Zhōngguó	China
中年	zhōngnián	middle age
中文	Zhōngwén	Chinese language
中心	zhōngxīn	center
中學	zhōngxué	middle school

stroke order:

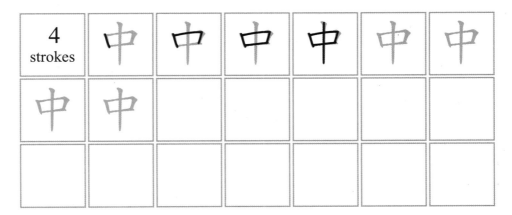

4 strokes

东
dōng　　　east

ㄉㄨㄥ

evolution:

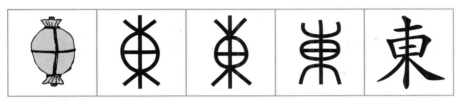

The character originally indicated a kind of bag which had two ends tied, but it became a loan character for "east".

examples:

東北　　　dōngběi　　　northeast

東方　　　dōngfāng　　　east; oriental

東南　　　dōngnán　　　southeast

東西　　　dōngxī　　　east and west

東西　　　dōngxi　　　thing

stroke order:

8 strokes	東	東	東	東	東	東
東	東	東	東	東	東	

西　xī　west

T
ˉ

evolution:

The old form depicted a bird sitting in a nest. Since birds roost in their nests when the sun sets in the west, this character came to mean "west".

examples:

西ˉ北ˇ	xīběi	northwest
西ˉ餐ㄘㄢ	xīcān	Western food
西ˉ服ㄈㄨˊ	xīfú	Western suit
西ˉ瓜ㄍㄨㄚ	xīguā	watermelon
西ˉ南ㄋㄢˊ	xīnán	southwest

stroke order:

南　nán　south

ㄋ
ㄢˊ

evolution:

The character originally indicated an ancient musical instrument, but it came to mean "south".

examples:

南ㄋㄢˊ北ㄅㄟˇ	nánběi	north and south
南ㄋㄢˊ方ㄈㄤ	nánfāng	southern part; south
南ㄋㄢˊ瓜ㄍㄨㄚ	nánguā	pumpkin
南ㄋㄢˊ極ㄐㄧˊ	nánjí	the South pole
南ㄋㄢˊ緯ㄨㄟˇ	nánwěi	the south latitude

stroke order:

9 strokes	南	南	南	南	南	南
南	南	南	南	南	南	南

běi   north

ㄅㄟˇ

evolution:

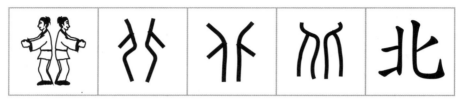

The character depicts two men standing back to back. The original meaning was "back", but the current meaning is "north".

examples:

北ㄅㄟˇ邊ㄅㄧㄢ	běibiān	north
北ㄅㄟˇ方ㄈㄤ	běifāng	northern part; north
北ㄅㄟˇ極ㄐㄧˊ	běijí	the North Pole
北ㄅㄟˇ極ㄐㄧˊ星ㄒㄧㄥ	běijíxīng	the North Star
北ㄅㄟˇ緯ㄨㄟˇ	běiwěi	the north latitude

stroke order:

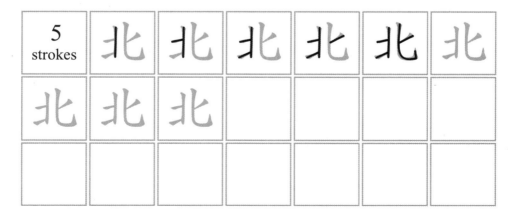

5 strokes

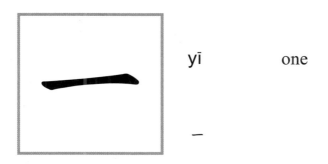

yī   one

一

evolution:

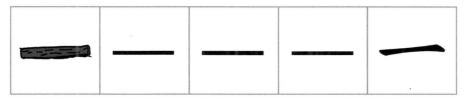

A horizontal stroke indicates "one".

examples:

一 流	yīliú	first-class; first-rate
第 一	dìyī	first
十 一	shíyī	eleven
萬 一	wànyī	in case
星 期 一	xīngqíyī	Monday

stroke order:

1 stroke	—	—	—	—	—	

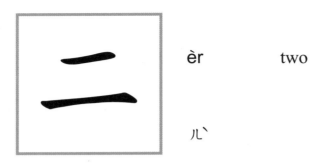

èr   two

ㄦˋ

evolution:

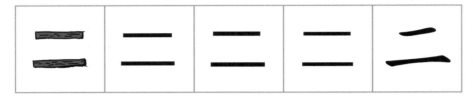

Two horizontal strokes indicate "two".

examples:

二ㄦˋ月ㄩㄝˋ	èryuè	February
第ㄉㄧˋ二ㄦˋ	dì'èr	second
十ㄕˊ二ㄦˋ	shí'èr	twelve
十ㄕˊ二ㄦˋ月ㄩㄝˋ	shí'èryuè	December
星ㄒㄧㄥ期ㄑㄧˊ二ㄦˋ	xīngqí'èr	Tuesday

stroke order:

2 strokes	一	二	二	二	二	二

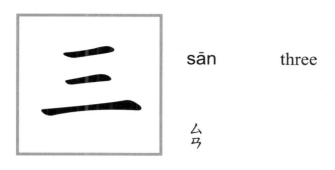

sān   three

ㄙㄢ

evolution:

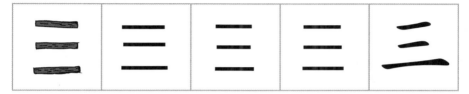

Three horizontal strokes indicate "three".

examples:

三ㄙㄢ角ㄐㄧㄠˇ	sānjiǎo	triangle
三ㄙㄢ十ㄕˊ	sānshí	thirty
三ㄙㄢ月ㄩㄝˋ	sānyuè	March
十ㄕˊ三ㄙㄢ	shísān	thirteen
星ㄒㄧㄥ期ㄑㄧˊ三ㄙㄢ	xīngqísān	Wednesday

stroke order:

3 stroke	三	三	三	三	三	三
三						

 sì four

ㄙˋ

evolution:

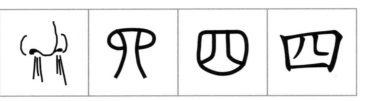

The original form resembled a breathing nose, meaning "breath", but this character came to mean "four".

examples:

四ㄙˋ處ㄔㄨˋ	sìchù	around; everywhere
四ㄙˋ季ㄐㄧˋ	sìjì	the four seasons
四ㄙˋ面ㄇㄧㄢˋ	sìmiàn	four sides; all sides
四ㄙˋ月ㄩㄝˋ	sìyuè	April
十ㄕˊ四ㄙˋ	shísì	fourteen

stroke order:

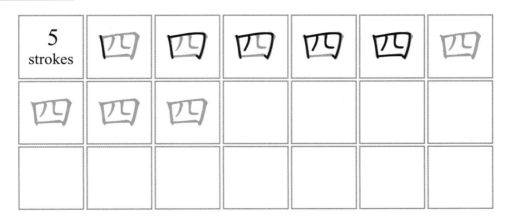

5 strokes

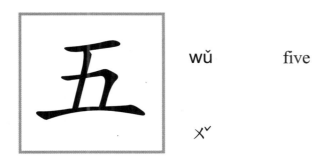

wǔ　　　five

ㄨˇ

evolution:

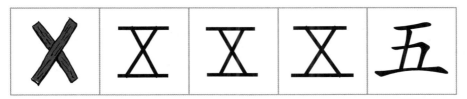

The old form of this character looked like a cross, which signified "five" in ancient China.

examples:

五ㄨˇ官ㄍㄨㄢ	wǔguān	the five sense organs
五ㄨˇ百ㄅㄞˇ	wǔbǎi	five hundred
五ㄨˇ十ㄕˊ	wǔshí	fifty
五ㄨˇ月ㄩㄝˋ	wǔyuè	May
十ㄕˊ五ㄨˇ	shíwǔ	fifteen

stroke order:

4 stroke	五	五	五	五	五	五
五	五					

六　　　liù　　　six

ㄌㄧㄡˋ

evolution:

The character originally indicated a shabby hut, but it came to mean "six".

examples:

六百	liùbǎi	six hundred
六千	liùqiān	six thousand
六十	liùshí	sixty
六月	liùyuè	June
十六	shíliù	sixteen

stroke order:

4 strokes	六	六	六	六	六	六
六	六					

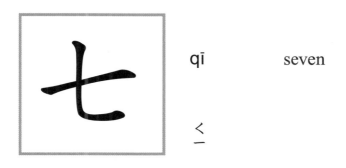

qī   seven

く
一

evolution:

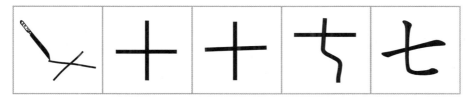

The original form depicted two cuts made by a knife. This character originally meant "to cut", but it became a loan character for "seven".

examples:

七百	qībǎi	seven hundred
七千	qīqiān	seven thousand
七十	qīshí	seventy
第七	dìqī	seventh
十七	shíqī	seventeen

stroke order:

2 strokes	七	七	七	七	七	七

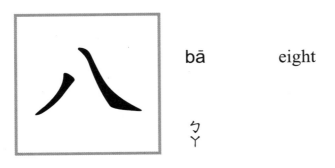

八   bā   eight

ㄅ
ㄚ

evolution:

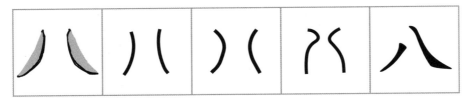

This character originally meant "to divide", but it came to mean "eight". The character 分 "to divide" (see p. 75) still keeps the radical 八 "eight" on top.

examples:

八百	bābǎi	eight hundred
八千	bāqiān	eight thousand
八十	bāshí	eighty
第八	dìbā	eighth
十八	shíbā	eighteen

stroke order:

2 strokes	八	八	八	八	八	八

九　　jiǔ　　　nine

ㄐㄧㄡˇ

evolution:

This character originally meant "elbow", but it came to mean "nine".

examples:

九千	jiǔqiān	nine thousand
九十	jiǔshí	ninety
九月	jiǔyuè	September
第九	dìjiǔ	ninth
十九	shíjiǔ	nineteen

stroke order:

2 strokes	九	九	九	九	九	九

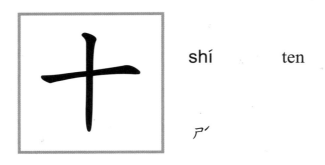

shí   ten

ㄕˊ

evolution:

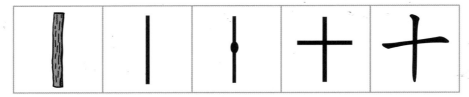

The number "ten" was originally depicted as a vertical stroke.

examples:

十ㄕˊ分ㄈㄣ	shífēn	very; extremely
十ㄕˊ萬ㄨㄢˋ	shíwàn	a hundred thousand
十ㄕˊ一ㄧ月ㄩㄝˋ	shíyīyuè	November
十ㄕˊ月ㄩㄝˋ	shíyuè	October
二ㄦˋ十ㄕˊ	èrshí	twenty

stroke order:

2 strokes	十	十	十	十	十	十

PART 3

TEST YOURSELF
(MATCHING EXERCISES & PINYIN PRACTICE)

EXERCISE 1: Match each picture with its character and fill in the blank with its meaning(s).

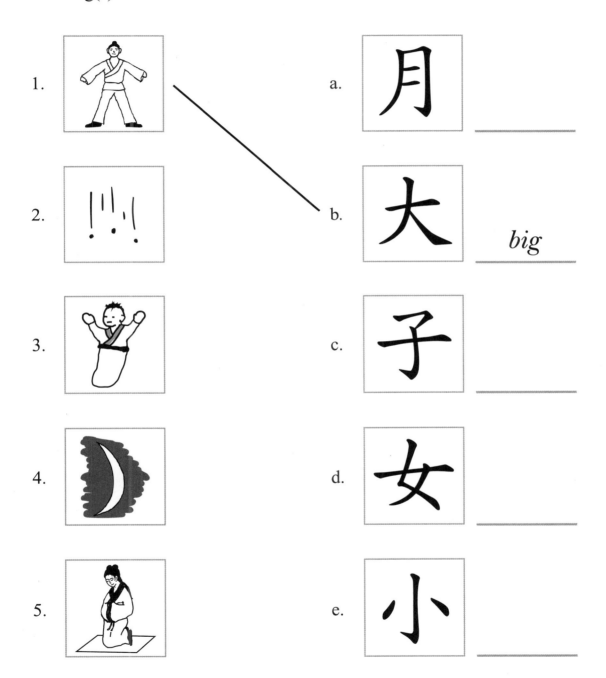

1.

2.

3.

4.

5.

a. 月 ___

b. 大 ___ *big*

c. 子 ___

d. 女 ___

e. 小 ___

EXERCISE 2: Circle the correct Hanyu Pinyin.

1. 人　　a. jié　b. huà　c. rén　d. shǎo

2. 大　　a. liàng　b. dà　c. duō　d. jiǎn

3. 天　　a. jiān　b. tiān　c. méi　d. hěn

4. 日　　a. rì　b. bàn　c. hǎo　d. shū

5. 月　　a. liù　b. yě　c. xiàn　d. yuè

6. 明　　a. míng　b. chǎng　c. zhui　d. běn

7. 女　　a. shì　b. fǎng　c. nǚ　d. qiān

8. 子　　a. téng　b. xìng　c. zǐ　d. hǒng

9. 好　　a. hǎo　b. kōng　c. huàng　d. kàn

10. 小　　a. jīn　b. xiǎo　c. wén　d. yào

EXERCISE 1:
1. b / big
2. e / small
3. c / son; child
4. a / the moon; month
5. d / woman; female; girl

EXERCISE 2:
1. c　　6. a
2. b　　7. c
3. b　　8. c
4. a　　9. a
5. d　　10. b

EXERCISE 1: Match each picture with its character and fill in the blank with its meaning(s).

1.

a.  ____

2.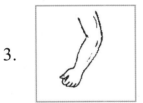

b. 田 ____

3.

c.  ____

4.

d.  ____

5.

e. 休 ____

EXERCISE 2: Circle the correct Hanyu Pinyin.

1. 少   a. jié   b. shǎo   c. rén   d. nuǎn

2. 多   a. liàng   b. tā   c. duō   d. mèi

3. 木   a. jiān   b. tiān   c. zhè   d. mù

4. 林   a. diè   b. lín   c. hǎo   d. shū

5. 休   a. liù   b. xiū   c. xiàn   d. yuan

6. 本   a. míng   b. shēng   c. zhui   d. běn

7. 果   a. shì   b. guǒ   c. liāng   d. pào

8. 李   a. téng   b. xìng   c. lǐ   d. zhōng

9. 田   a. chǔ   b. kōng   c. huàng   d. tiān

10. 力   a. lì   b. xiǎo   c. wén   d. kē

answers

EXERCISE 1:
1. c / fruit; as expected
2. a / wood; tree
3. d / force; strength
4. b / field
5. e / rest; cease

EXERCISE 2:
1. b   6. d
2. c   7. b
3. d   8. c
4. b   9. d
5. b   10. a

EXERCISE 1: Match each picture with its character and fill in the blank with its meaning(s).

1.

a.

2.

b.

3.

c.

4.

d.

5.

e.

EXERCISE 2: Circle the correct Hanyu Pinyin.

1. 男　a. jié　b. shǎo　c. nán　d. nuǎn

2. 文　a. liàng　b. fēng　c. duō　d. wén

3. 交　a. jiān　b. jiāo　c. zhè　d. lì

4. 立　a. dǎn　b. yǒng　c. lì　d. zhuāng

5. 夫　a. fū　b. liàn　c. xiàn　d. jiān

6. 安　a. míng　b. qiáng　c. suo　d. ān

7. 字　a. zì　b. guǒ　c. liāng　d. dòng

8. 家　a. jiā　b. gé　c. xiào　d. gān

9. 父　a. fù　b. kōng　c. huàng　d. qìng

10. 母　a. gàn　b. mǔ　c. wén　d. shuǎng

answers

EXERCISE 1:
1. c / family; home
2. e / cross; hand over; associate with
3. d / mother
4. a / script; language; culture
5. b / peaceful; safe

EXERCISE 2:
1. c　　6. d
2. d　　7. a
3. b　　8. a
4. c　　9. a
5. a　　10. b

EXERCISE 1: Match each picture with its character and fill in the blank with its meaning(s).

1.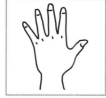

a.  ___

2.

b.  ___

3.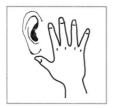

c.  ___

4.

d.  ___

5.

e.  ___

EXERCISE 2: Circle the correct Hanyu Pinyin.

1. 老　　a. lǎo　　b. shǎo　　c. mǎo　　d. nǎo

2. 手　　a. shǒu　　b. shàng　　c. shòu　　d. zài

3. 友　　a. wǎng　　b. jiào　　c. yǒu　　d. guān

4. 耳　　a. duì　　b. yī　　c. ěr　　d. tì

5. 取　　a. qǔ　　b. yǔ　　c. chèn　　d. cóng

6. 目　　a. kào　　b. mù　　c. dào　　d. ān

7. 看　　a. zì　　b. bā　　c. dà　　d. kàn

8. 相　　a. béi　　b. chū　　c. xiàng　　d. lài

9. 心　　a. qiáng　　b. xīn　　c. zhū　　d. yuè

10. 自　　a. gàn　　b. qiǎo　　c. huà　　d. zì

EXERCISE 1: Match each picture with its character and fill in the blank with its meaning(s).

1.

a.  _____

2.

b.  _____

3.

c.  _____

4.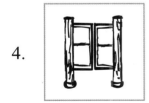

d.  _____

5.

e.  _____

EXERCISE 2: Circle the correct Hanyu Pinyin.

1. 身　a. shēn　b. shǎo　c. xié　d. fen

2. 口　a. liàng　b. kǒu　c. diǎn　d. bāng

3. 加　a. jiān　b. jiā　c. pái　d. dà

4. 如　a. duàn　b. rú　c. wō　d. tǒu

5. 合　a. xī　b. hé　c. wéi　d. fàn

6. 向　a. yòng　b. xiàng　c. hǎo　d. zhào

7. 門　a. rén　b. mén　c. diàn　d. xīn

8. 間　a. kè　b. wán　c. jiān　d. guāng

9. 問　a. guǒ　b. dōng　c. báng　d. wèn

10. 們　a. mì　b. xiàn　c. máo　d. men

answers

EXERCISE 1:
1. c / close; join
2. e / body
3. a / direction; facing; toward
4. b / door; gate
5. d / mouth; opening

EXERCISE 2:
1. a　　6. b
2. b　　7. b
3. b　　8. c
4. b　　9. d
5. b　　10. d

EXERCISE 1: Match each picture with its character and fill in the blank with its meaning(s).

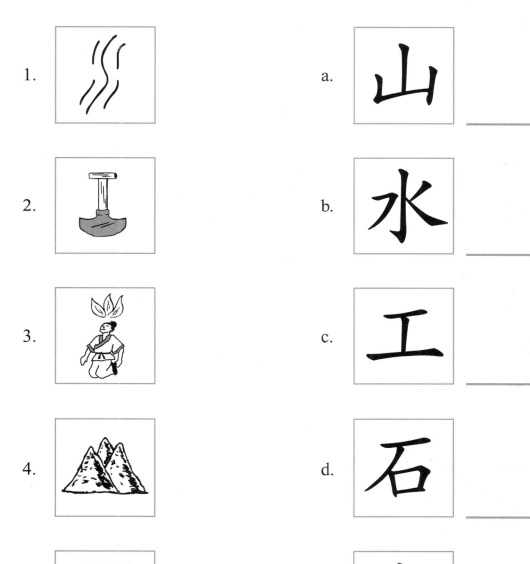

1.

a. 山 ____

2.

b. 水 ____

3.

c. 工 ____

4.

d. 石 ____

5.

e. 光 ____

EXERCISE 2: Circle the correct Hanyu Pinyin.

1. 工　　a. shēn　　b. shǎo　　c. gōng　　d. dǎ

2. 左　　a. pīng　　b. kǒu　　c. zuǒ　　d. bāng

3. 右　　a. yòu　　b. hóng　　c. pái　　d. zào

4. 上　　a. zhén　　b. shàng　　c. shà　　d. diàn

5. 下　　a. xià　　b. sāi　　c. wéi　　d. mǎo

6. 火　　a. yòng　　b. xiàng　　c. huǒ　　d. lǔ

7. 光　　a. mǎo　　b. guāng　　c. shú　　d. zhàng

8. 山　　a. gāo　　b. shān　　c. dào　　d. wǎn

9. 水　　a. mù　　b. dōng　　c. shuǐ　　d. chá

10. 石　　a. shí　　b. cǎo　　c. máo　　d. dāo

---

answers

EXERCISE 1:
1. b / water
2. c / work; industry
3. e / light; glory
4. a / mountain; hill
5. d / stone; rock

EXERCISE 2:
1. c	6. c
2. c	7. b
3. a	8. b
4. b	9. c
5. a	10. a

EXERCISE 1: Match each picture with its character and fill in the blank with its meaning(s).

1.

a. 魚 _____

2.

b. 象 _____

3.

c. 出 _____

4.

d. 去 _____

5.

e. 雨 _____

EXERCISE 2: Circle the correct Hanyu Pinyin.

1. 土   a. tǔ   b. shǎo   c. nán   d. chěng

2. 生   a. yì   b. shēng   c. sài   d. huà

3. 氣   a. jiān   b. fù   c. qì   d. jià

4. 雨   a. diàn   b. yǒng   c. yǔ   d. bǎn

5. 電   a. fū   b. diàn   c. liǔ   d. sháo

6. 魚   a. míng   b. qiáng   c. yú   d. mǎi

7. 馬   a. zì   b. guǒ   c. liāng   d. mǎ

8. 象   a. jiā   b. sān   c. xiàng   d. gān

9. 出   a. chū   b. kōng   c. lī   d. qìng

10. 去   a. gàn   b. mǔ   c. qíng   d. qù

answers

EXERCISE 1:
1. e / rain
2. a / fish
3. d / go; leave
4. b / elephant; appearance
5. c / go out; produce

EXERCISE 2:
1. a   6. c
2. b   7. d
3. c   8. c
4. c   9. a
5. b   10. d

EXERCISE 1: Match each picture with its character and fill in the blank with its meaning(s).

1.

a.  _____

2.

b.  _____

3.

c.  _____

4.

d.  _____

5.

e.  _____

EXERCISE 2: Circle the correct Hanyu Pinyin.

1. 行　　a. xíng　　b. huà　　c. rén　　d. shǎo

2. 回　　a. liàng　　b. huí　　c. duō　　d. jiǎn

3. 王　　a. wáng　　b. tiān　　c. méi　　d. hěn

4. 白　　a. bái　　b. bàn　　c. hǎo　　d. shū

5. 分　　a. fēn　　b. lái　　c. xiàn　　d. yuè

6. 衣　　a. yī　　b. chǎng　　c. qīn　　d. běn

7. 角　　a. shì　　b. fǎng　　c. jiǎo　　d. qiān

8. 高　　a. téng　　b. xìng　　c. gāo　　d. hǒng

9. 美　　a. hǎo　　b. kōng　　c. měi　　d. kàn

10. 買　　a. mǎi　　b. xiǎo　　c. wén　　d. yào

---

answers

EXERCISE 1:
1. e / king; (a surname)
2. c / divide; seperate
3. b / return; turn around
4. a / high; tall
5. d / beautiful

EXERCISE 2:
1. a　　6. a
2. b　　7. c
3. a　　8. c
4. a　　9. c
5. a　　10. a

EXERCISE 1: Match each picture with its character and fill in the blank with its meaning(s).

1.

a.  _____

2.

b.  _____

3.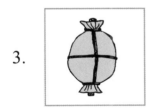

c.  _____

4.

d.  _____

5.

e.  _____

EXERCISE 2: Circle the correct Hanyu Pinyin.

1. 我　　a. shòu　　b. shǎo　　c. ér　　d. wǒ

2. 有　　a. liàng　　b. fēng　　c. xuě　　d. yǒu

3. 算　　a. suàn　　b. zhǎng　　c. zhè　　d. diào

4. 筆　　a. dǎn　　b. yǒng　　c. miàn　　d. bǐ

5. 教　　a. jiào　　b. liàng　　c. diǎn　　d. jiā

6. 中　　a. guān　　b. qiáng　　c. zhōng　　d. chá

7. 東　　a. lōng　　b. dōng　　c. cōng　　d. dòng

8. 西　　a. jiā　　b. xī　　c. xiào　　d. béi

9. 南　　a. fù　　b. còu　　c. nán　　d. qìng

10. 北　　a. xiǎo　　b. lǐng　　c. dàn　　d. běi

---

answers

EXERCISE 1:
1. c / calculate; count
2. b / north
3. a / east
4. e / teach; religion
5. d / middle; China

EXERCISE 2:
1. d　　6. c
2. d　　7. b
3. a　　8. b
4. d　　9. c
5. a　　10. d

EXERCISE 1: Match each picture with its character and fill in the blank with its meaning(s).

1.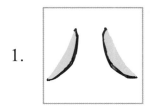

a.  _____

2.

b.  _____

3.

c.  _____

4.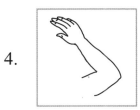

d.  _____

5.

e.  _____

EXERCISE 2: Circle the correct Hanyu Pinyin.

1. 一 a. shēn b. yī c. xié d. dīng

2. 二 a. liàng b. kǒu c. èr d. biǎo

3. 三 a. jiān b. sān c. pái d. dà

4. 四 a. mào b. rú c. sì d. jù

5. 五 a. zhào b. wǔ c. lái d. fàn

6. 六 a. liù b. xiàng c. hǎo d. zhào

7. 七 a. qī b. mén c. diàn d. xīn

8. 八 a. bā b. bàn c. jiān d. bǎo

9. 九 a. táng b. fǎ c. jiǔ d. bèn

10. 十 a. shù b. shí c. shǐ d. shī

PART
4

CD-ROM GUIDELINES

A Multimedia Self-Learning Course

CHINESE CHARACTERS FOR BEGINNERS is an ideal introduction to the Chinese language for beginners or for those who have a basic knowledge of Chinese. Using computer-based graphics, sound and animation, this program lets users explore Chinese characters with great fun. It covers frequently used characters, words and phrases. In addition to providing practice, the games and exercises are designed to be challenging. This program provides a dynamic environment that is both educational and fun.

SYSTEM REQUIREMENTS

* Windows 95/98/2000/Me/XP
* Pentium 233 or higher
* 32 MB RAM or higher
* 16-speed CD-ROM drive or higher
* SVGA card and monitor
  (capable of 640*480 resolution with 24 bit color)
* 16 bit MPC compatible sound card
* mouse & speaker

INSTALLATION

This program contains an auto-run installation. Just insert the CD-ROM disc into your CD-ROM drive and let it run automatically.

In case it doesn't run:
1. Double click on the **My Computer** icon.
2. Double click on your CD-ROM drive icon.
3. Double Click on the **Panda (Chinese)** icon.

GETTING STARTED

Main Menu
The Main Menu contains three choices: **Introduction to Chinese Characters**, **Learning Chinese Characters**, and **Games and Exercises**.

A. Introduction to Chinese Characters

There are 10 pages in this section. Click on **next** to go to the next page and click on **previous** to return to the previous page.

B. Learning Chinese Characters

There are 4 pages (100 characters) in this section. Click on the characters to enter each lesson. It is suggested that you learn the characters from right to left, top to bottom, since the characters progress from simple to complex in this order.

Each lesson contains:
the traditional character (as used in Taiwan)
the simplified character (as used in China and Singapore)
Mandarin Phonetic Symbols (as used in Taiwan)
Hanyu Pinyin (as used in China and Singapore)
meaning(s)
pronunciation (click on **pronunciation**)
origin (click on **origin**)
stroke order (click on **stroke order**)
examples (click on **examples**)

C. Games and Exercises

The **Games and Exercises** section aims to test the user's comprehension of the 100 characters and 500 words and phrases learned in the **Learning Chinese Characters** section. The **Memory Game** is to test the user's recognition of the characters. The **Stroke Game** is to test the user's comprehension of the number of strokes of each character. The **Listening Comprehension** is to test the user's comprehension of the examples and their pronunciation.

1. Memory Game

Objective: To test the user's recognition of the characters.
Directions: Click on two cards to match the characters.

2. Stroke Game

Objective: To test the user's comprehension of the number of strokes of each character.
Directions: Click on the number to indicate the correct number of strokes of each character.

3. Listening Comprehension

Objective: To test the user's comprehension of the examples and their pronunciation.
Directions: Listen to the pronunciation and click on the correct word or phrase.

CONTACT US

PANDA MEDIA CO., LTD.
Address: 3F, No.153, Ting Chow Rd.
Sec.3, Taipei, Taiwan, R.O.C. 100
Tel: 886-2-2365-3976
Fax: 886-2-2369-1206
E-mail: pandamedia@seed.net.tw